Sean Price

Chicago, Illinois

© 2008 Raintree
Published by Raintree,
A division of Reed Elsevier Inc.
Chicago, Illinois

Customer Service: **888-454-2279**

Visit our website at **www.raintreelibrary.com**

Designed by Kimberly R. Miracle and Betsy Wernert
Photo Research by Tracy Cummins
Map on page 7 by Mapping Specialists
Printed in China by Leo Paper Group

11 10 09 08 07
10 9 8 7 6 5 4 3 2 1

Library of Congress Cataloging-in-Publication Data
Price, Sean.
  Route 66 : America's road / Sean Price.
      p. cm. -- (American history through primary sources)
  Includes bibliographical references and index.
  ISBN-13: 978-1-4109-2697-5 (hb)
  ISBN-13: 978-1-4109-2708-8 (pb)
  1. United States Highway 66--History--Juvenile literature. 2. Automobile travel--United States--History--20th century--Juvenile literature. 3. United States Highway 66--Juvenile literature. 4. United States--Description and travel--Juvenile literature. I. Title. II. Title: Route sixty six.
  HE356.U55P75 2008
  388.1'220973--dc22

                    2007008260

Acknowledgments
The author and publisher are grateful to the following for permission to reproduce copyright material: Bettmann/CORBIS **pp.5, 24**; Curt Teich Postcard Archives Lake County Discovery Museum **pp. 6, 8, 9**; Natalia Bratslavsky / Alamy **p. 10 top**; Joseph Scherschel//Time Life Pictures/Getty Images **pp. 10 bottom, 11**; Leland J. Prater/Corbis **12 top**; Andreas Feininger/Time Life Pictures/Getty Images **pp. 12–13**; Library of Congress Prints and Photographs Division **p. 15**; Nik Wheeler/CORBIS **p. 16**; ROBYN BECK/AFP/Getty Images **pp. 18, 21**; AP Photo **p. 19**; Tom Bean/Getty Images **p. 20**; Hulton Archive/Getty Images **p. 22**; Gene Lester/Getty Images **p. 23**; JP Laffont/Sygma/Corbis **pp. 26–27**; Franck Fotos/Alamy **pp. 28–29**.

Cover Image reproduced with the permission of Bettmann/CORBIS.

The publishers would like to thank Nancy Harris for her assistance in the preparation of this book.

Disclaimer
All the Internet addresses (URLs) given in this book were valid at the time of going to press. However, due to the dynamic nature of the Internet, some addresses may have changed, or sites may have changed or ceased to exist since publication. While the author and publishers regret any inconvenience this may cause readers, no responsibility for any such changes can be accepted by either the author or the publishers.

Contents

Some words are printed in bold, **like this**. You can find out what they mean on page 30. You can also look in the box at the bottom of the page where they first appear.

Main Street of America

Cars were new in the early 1900s. Few people owned them. Cars cost a lot of money. People walked instead of driving. They rode horses or bicycles. On long trips, they could take trains. But they could only go where the trains went. Trains did not go everywhere. It was hard for most people to travel long distances.

In 1905, Americans owned just 79,000 cars. By 1916, there were 9 million cars in the United States. These new drivers faced a big problem. The U.S. did not have many **paved** roads. Paved roads have a hard, smooth surface. Most paved roads were in cities.

The U.S. began building paved roads. Many of them were **highways**. Highways are large roads. They connect towns and cities. U.S. Highway 66 was one of the longest roads. People called it Route 66. A route was another name for a highway. Route 66 became very popular. People still call it the "Main Street of America."

This is an ad for a new Ford car. It is from 1930. It shows that traveling in cars was exciting. It's not a good idea to feed bears, though!

paved   covered with a hard, smooth surface
highway   large roads that connect cities and towns

Building Route 66

Building Route 66 began in 1926. But it was not totally paved until 1938. Route 66 was 2,448 miles long. It started in Chicago, Illinois. It ended at Santa Monica, California. That is near Los Angeles. (See map on the right.) Many smaller cities and towns were in between.

This postcard shows the path that Route 66 cut across the United States. You can compare it to the real map to the right.

Map labels:

N W E S

Lake Michigan

Chicago

Great Salt Lake

St. Louis

Grand Canyon

Meramec Caves

Barstow

San Bernardino · Kingman

Petrified Forest

Gallup

Blue Whale

Joplin

Oklahoma City

Catoosa

Rialto

Santa Monica Beach/Pier · Los Angeles

Winona · Flagstaff

Holbrook

Amarillo

Cadillac Ranch

PACIFIC OCEAN

0   250   500 miles

0   250   500 kilometers

Gulf of Mexico

Route 66 was an important road. It allowed people to drive quickly to the West Coast. They could also drive back quickly. The highway crossed many plains and deserts. Much of that ground was flat. Trucks are easier to drive in flat areas. They carry heavy loads. So truck drivers liked Route 66.

Car drivers liked it, too. Traffic on Route 66 grew. Route 66 was mostly a two-lane road. Over time, it became wider in some places. That allowed more cars to travel on it.

States crossed by Route 66

Illinois
Missouri
Kansas
Oklahoma
Texas
New Mexico
Arizona
California

7

Sights to see

Route 66 helped people travel. Drivers could stop wherever they wanted. They could see new places. Route 66 took them through many natural wonders. A natural wonder has odd or beautiful sights.

Some of the places they could visit on Route 66 were:

Meramec Caverns

These are underground caves in Missouri. Native Americans used these caves for shelter. So did Jesse James. He was a famous bank robber.

↑ Meramec Caverns

Petrified Forest

This is a national park. It is in Arizona. It has beautiful rocks and hills. Many rocks were once pieces of wood. But they became **petrified**. That means they turned to stone. This takes millions of years.

Petrified Forest

petrified   turned to stone

Grand Canyon

This is also a national park. It is also in Arizona. The canyon is a huge, wide cut in the ground. People can hike in it. They can raft on the river in it. They can camp in it, too!

Grand Canyon

H.1541. TOP OF RED SANDSTONE CLIFFS ON HERMIT TRAIL, GRAND CANYON NATION

Santa Monica Beach

This is in California. It has great weather all year. Families swim in the ocean and enjoy the beach. There is also an amusement park.

SM-32 LOOKING TOWARDS OCEAN PARK FROM BEACH CLUBS, SANTA MONICA, CALIFORNIA

Santa Monica Beach

You can find these places on the map on page 7.

Road signs

Americans built more roads starting in the 1920s. So companies put up **ads** along those roads. Ads are signs that tell us about a product, such as a new soft drink. Many ads were put on giant signs called **billboards**.

Phillips 66

In 1927, the Phillips **Petroleum** (oil) Company was in Oklahoma. The company made its gas near Route 66. The road was very popular. So the company called its gas Phillips 66. Phillips 66 is still used today.

Ads gave bored drivers something to read. Many drivers liked Burma-Shave ads. Burma-Shave was a type of shaving cream. Each Burma-Shave ad was a short poem. The poem was put onto five different red signs. These signs were spread out over many miles. A final sign always said "Burma-Shave."

Burma-Shave ad:
The little Burma-Shave poems were usually funny or cute. Here's an example.

Sign 1: **Highways are**

Sign 2: **No place to sleep**

Sign 3: **Stop your car**

Sign 4: **To count your sheep**

Sign 5: **Burma-Shave**

These people are making baskets from strips of white oak. The baskets will be sold as souvenirs on Route 66.

souver
trading po

Places to stop

Many different shops appeared along Route 66. They sold **souvenirs**. Souvenirs remind people of things they have done. People could buy pieces of **petrified** wood. This is wood that has turned to stone. Visitors could also buy toys.

Route 66 crossed land owned by Native Americans. Travelers wanted to see native dances and costumes. Many **trading posts** were set up on Route 66. Trading posts were stores that sold things made by Native Americans. They sold blankets and jewelry. They also sold food and gas.

Many restaurants became popular with travelers. Some restaurants cooked homemade food. Others made "fast food."

The very first McDonald's was near Route 66. It was set up in 1939. At first, McDonald's was a regular restaurant. But by 1948, McDonald's began making low-cost food fast. The idea quickly caught on.

Drivers stopped for gas at the many towns along Route 66. They could also get something to eat. If they were tired, they could stay the night.

Moving West

In the 1930s, **drought** hit the United States. A drought is a lack of rain. The drought caused dust storms. These storms blew through many states. The storms were strongest in Oklahoma, Kansas, Texas, Colorado, and New Mexico. People called this area the Dust Bowl (see map below).

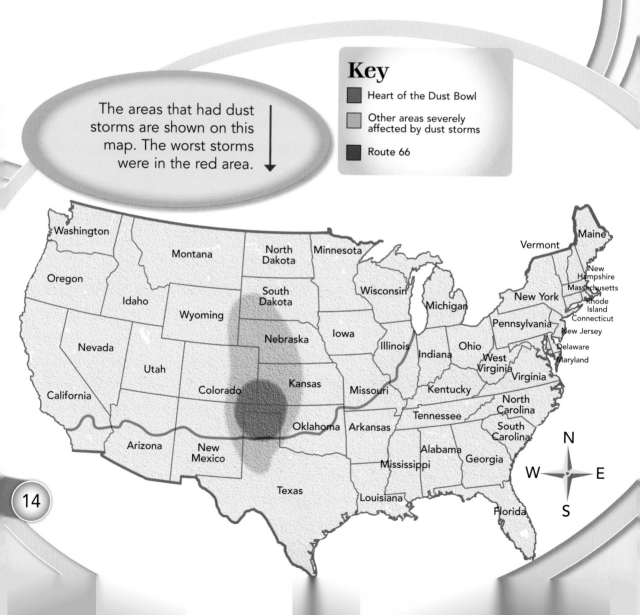

The areas that had dust storms are shown on this map. The worst storms were in the red area.

Key

- Heart of the Dust Bowl
- Other areas severely affected by dust storms
- Route 66

Okies packed all that they had onto cars like this one.

Dust storms destroyed crops on farms. The farmers had to move. They drove to California to find jobs. Most drove on Route 66.

A lot of these people were poor. Many were from Oklahoma. People leaving the Dust Bowl were known as **Okies**. John Steinbeck wrote a book about the Okies. The story was made-up. But it was based on things that really happened. The story was called *The Grapes of Wrath*.

Steinbeck called Route 66 the "Mother Road." That was because smaller roads led to Route 66. Route 66 is still called the Mother Road.

Parts of Route 66 could be dangerous. Drivers had to be careful.

slaughter   kill
military   soldiers, sailors, and pilots who fight in wars

Deadly curves

More and more people drove on Route 66. But there were problems with the road. It had many tight turns. People sometimes drove too fast. They had accidents at those turns. Many were hurt. Others died. One part of Route 66 was known as "**Slaughter** Lane." Slaughter means to kill. Some of these areas were changed. Tight curves were made straight. Route 66 became safer to drive.

Route 66 at war

The United States entered World War II in 1941. The war cut down on traffic. People could not buy gasoline. Gas was needed to fight the war.

The **military** did have gasoline. The military is made up of people who fight in wars. The military used Route 66 a lot more during the war. The highway was used to move guns and other supplies.

The End of the Road?

World War II ended in 1945. After the war, more and more Americans bought cars. They needed wider highways. Wider roads could carry more cars.

In 1956, the U.S. created the **interstate** highway system. Interstate means between states. These roads were wider. There were also more of these roads. People could go to more places. President Dwight D. Eisenhower pushed the interstate highway plan. Eisenhower was the leader of the United States.

interstate   large highway. It usually runs through several states.

Workers take down the Route 66 sign in Chicago. An interstate replaced the highway.

The Will Rogers Highway

In 1952, Route 66 was named the Will Rogers Highway. Will Rogers was a famous American actor. He died in 1935. He was born near Claremont, Oklahoma. It is on Route 66.

Route 66 went through many small towns. Travelers had to slow down or stop at these towns. The towns had restaurants for travelers. They had hotels, too. But the new interstate highways were different. People could travel on them without stopping. This let them travel faster. People no longer came to the small towns on Route 66. Times were hard for these towns.

Tepee hotels

Route 66 once had several hotels that looked like **tepees** (see below.) Most have been torn down. Once Route 66 was replaced, not many people stayed in them. Only two of these hotels stayed in business. One is in Holbrook, Arizona. The other is in Rialto, California. (See the map on page 7.) They remain very popular.

↑ These "tepees" are really hotel rooms!

tepee   cone-shaped tent used by Native Americans

Bigger Highways

It took many years to replace Route 66. Building new interstate highways costs a lot of money. It also takes time. The new interstates did not follow Route 66 exactly. Some parts of Route 66 were torn up. Other parts were closed off. In other parts, a wider interstate highway took its place.

The last part of Route 66 was replaced in 1984. But pieces of the old road remain. Some parts are used by cities or states. They are the same road. But they have new names. Old stores and hotels still remain, too. Many people still like to visit them.

This piece of Route 66 is falling apart. ↓

A Famous Road

In 1946, Bobby Troup traveled on Route 66. He was a music writer. His wife said he should write a new song. She came up with the title. "Get your **kicks** on Route 66." That means "have fun on Route 66." Troup's new song became a hit. Traveling on Route 66 really was fun for people. The song showed how they felt.

People enjoyed Route 66 for many reasons. One of the biggest was that it showed them new and different places. A part of the song goes:

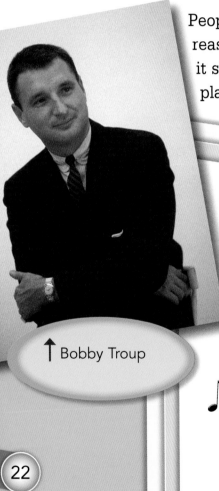

↑ Bobby Troup

Get Your Kicks on Route 66

*You go through St. Louis,
Joplin, Missouri, Oklahoma City
looks mighty **purty** (pretty)
You'll see Amarillo, Gallup, New Mexico
Flagstaff, Arizona, and don't forget Winona
Kingman, Barstow, San Bernardino*

All of these are cities and towns on Route 66. See if you can find them on the map on page 7.

22

---

kicks   another way to say "fun"
purty   another way of saying "pretty"

The Nat King Cole Trio recorded the song in 1946. It was a huge radio hit.

Route 66 on TV

Route 66 was the name of a TV show. The show focused on two young men. They drove around the United States. One was Tod Stiles. The other was Buz Murdock. Tod and Buz drove a Corvette. It is a type of sports car. The show made Corvettes more popular.

In the TV show, Tod and Buz traveled a lot. They met new people. They often helped those in trouble. The show discussed serious subjects. One show might be about growing up without parents. But the shows could be funny, too. *Route 66* was on TV from 1960 to 1964. Oddly, very little of the show was filmed on Route 66.

Route 66 in TV and film

More recent TV shows have used Route 66 in their stories. They include *Rugrats* and *Stargate SG-1*. The Disney movie *Cars* was also set on Route 66.

This photo is of the actors who played Tod Stiles and Buz Murdock in the TV show,

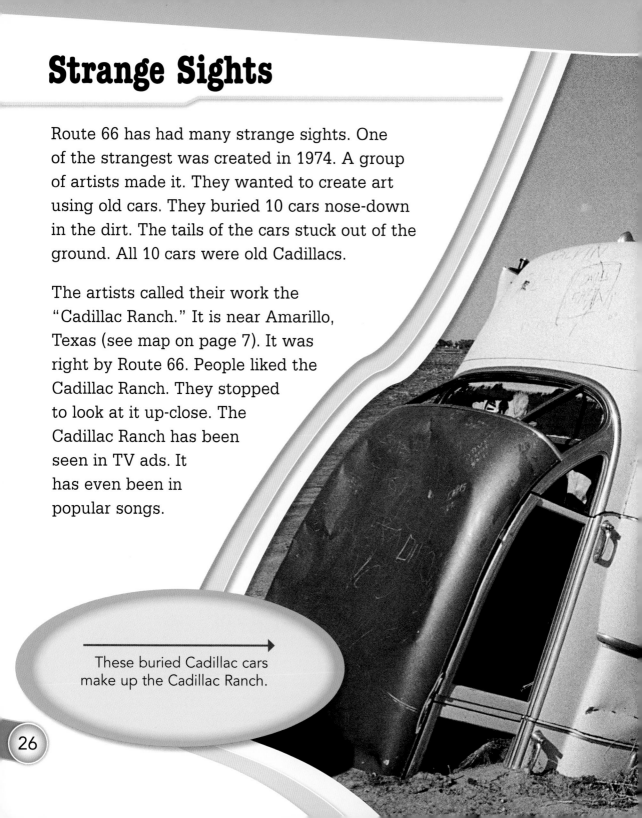

Strange Sights

Route 66 has had many strange sights. One of the strangest was created in 1974. A group of artists made it. They wanted to create art using old cars. They buried 10 cars nose-down in the dirt. The tails of the cars stuck out of the ground. All 10 cars were old Cadillacs.

The artists called their work the "Cadillac Ranch." It is near Amarillo, Texas (see map on page 7). It was right by Route 66. People liked the Cadillac Ranch. They stopped to look at it up-close. The Cadillac Ranch has been seen in TV ads. It has even been in popular songs.

These buried Cadillac cars make up the Cadillac Ranch.

The Cadillac Ranch is still by the old Route 66. But the road has a new name. It is Interstate 40. People still like to drive on the road. They like to see what was on Route 66.

The Blue Whale is still smiling. ↓
It is near Catoosa, Oklahoma. →

The Blue Whale

Oklahoma is not near the ocean (see map on page 7). But it has its very own whale! The Blue Whale can be found on Route 66. It is near the small town of Catoosa. The whale is made of concrete. It was part of a small water park.

The Blue Whale was built in the 1970s. A man named Hugh Davis made it. Kids jumped off the whale into the pond. It was first built for local kids. But many travelers on Route 66 stopped to swim, too. The Blue Whale became famous.

Davis had to close the water park in the late 1980s. He grew old. He could not keep running the park. The Blue Whale was no longer used. But in 2002, local groups fixed up the whale. People can no longer swim there. But they can picnic and take walks. The Blue Whale remains one of Route 66's best-known sights.

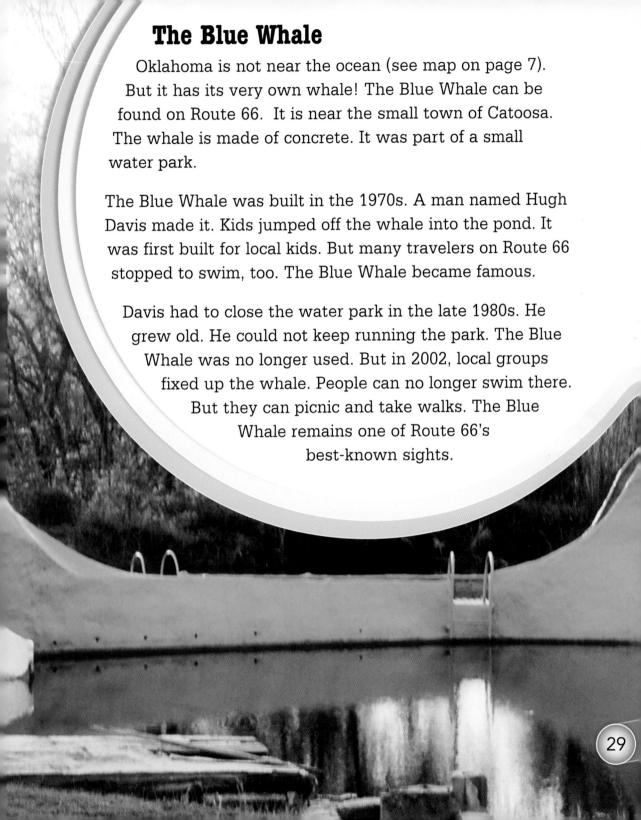

Glossary

ad
sign that tell about a product

billboard
giant sign

drought
lack of rain

Dust Bowl
U.S. dust storms in the 1930s

highway
large roads that connect cities and towns

interstate
large highway. It usually runs through several states.

kicks
another way to say "fun"

military
soldiers, sailors, and pilots who fight in wars

Okies
people who left the Dust Bowl. Many were from Oklahoma.

paved
covered with a hard, smooth surface

petrified
turned to stone

petroleum
oil

purty
another way of saying "pretty"

slaughter
to kill

souvenir
object that reminds someone of past events

tepee
cone-shaped tent used by Native Americans

trading post
type of store

Want to Know More?

Books to read

- Keating, Frank and Mike Wimmer. *Will Rogers: An American Legend.* San Diego: Silver Whistle, 2002.
- Petersen, David. *Grand Canyon: National Park.* Danbury, CT: Children's Press, 2001.
- Secakuku, Susan. *Meet Mindy: A Native Girl from the Southwest.* Hillsboro, OR: Beyond Words, 2002.

Websites

- http://americanhistory.si.edu/onthemove/exhibition/exhibition_10_1.html
  Visit this website by the National Museum of American History to find out more about Route 66's rich history.
- http://www.oklahomaroute66.com/
  This website can help guide you to the many interesting places on Route 66.

Places to visit

- **Petrified Forest National Park**
  Between the towns of Navajo and Holbrook in Arizona on Interstate 40 (Exit 311) (928) 524-6228 *Visit one of the most colorful national parks and see fossils from the dawn of the dinosaurs.*

- **Meramec Caverns**
  In Stanton, Missouri, on Interstate 44 (Exit 230) (800) 676-6105
  This system of caves takes visitors through 400 million years of history, including visits from the bank robber Jesse James and Hollywood stars.

Read *The Dirty Thirties: Documenting the Dust Bowl* to learn about the dust storms that swept across the midwestern United States during the 1930s.

Index